Bicky Becomes A Butterfly
I don't want to !

demigail PUBLISHING

read just the top, or read the top and bottom. . . and
when you're done, read the details of the butterfly
life cycle at the end of the book. . .eNjoy the story !

For every First Grader
You are amazing as you begin to read !

A
DEMIGAIL PUBLISHING
"emerging reader" book
www.demigail.com
Broadway, VA 22815

1463776624
ISBN: 978-1463776626

Bicky knew it was time.

His mother did not tell him. His father did not tell him.
His grandma did not tell him.
His grandpa did not tell him.
No one told Bicky it was time; but he knew.

1

The shell was so thin. . .

Bicky was crowded and cramped.
In the many days since the egg was laid,
he grew and grew.
He found he could no longer turn around.

2

sky-light came right in.

At the start, the egg was thick and opaque.
Bicky could not see out and no one could see in.
Now the egg is thin and sheer.
Bicky can see out and we can see in.

3

"I don't want to," Bicky said loudly.

It felt good to say how he felt out loud.
It actually made him feel quite proud.
But the words stayed in,
and simply echoed again and again.

4

No one heard because Bicky was alone in the shell.

The shell might be thin, but nothing could get out or in.
Alone, Bicky got lonely.
The shell was still strong, so nothing could go wrong.
Growing, Bicky was crowded.

5

With hope that someone out in the light would hear and come to help. . . .

Bicky knew that help was a tricky thing.
Sometimes you got what you desired.
Sometimes you got advice that made you tired.

Bicky gave a shout:
"I don't want to go out!"

That was how he really felt.
Right or wrong, it didn't matter because the feelings were real and inside of him.
Going out was scary and he just didn't want to do it.

No one came to help.

Bicky really wanted help now.
His head was pressed up to the shell and he felt stuck.
His back end was bending and his whole body felt tight.
He could see out, but no one was there.

Bicky had to stay inside the shell.

It was his choice to stay.
There seemed no other way.
He wriggled and curled to make some room.
The space he made would be gone real soon.

After a while,
it got hot inside the shell.

With the shell so thin, the sun came right in,
and made it really hot.
Bicky could not sweat, because caterpillars do not.
He began to feel like he was cooking in a pot.

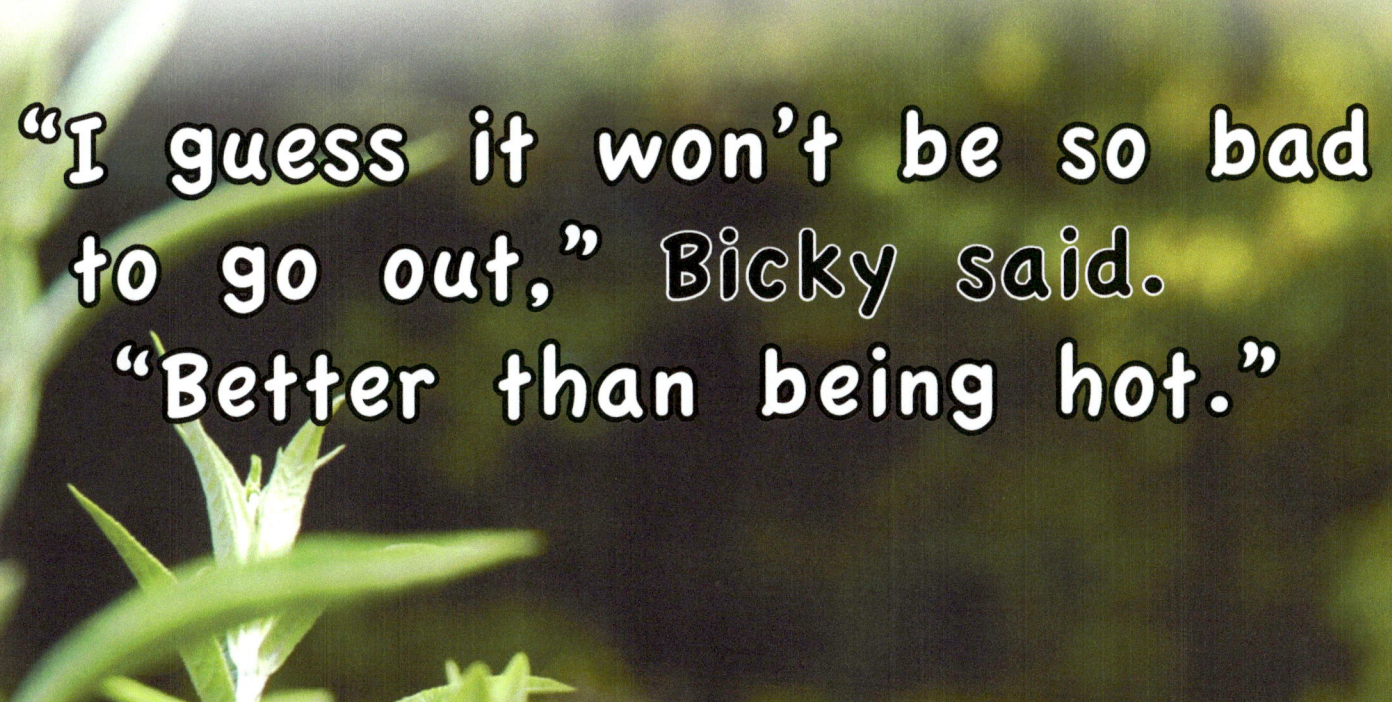

"I guess it won't be so bad to go out," Bicky said. "Better than being hot."

It was no longer a choice to stay inside the shell.
If Bicky did not go out, he would melt.
He looked toward the outside and saw things moving like there was a breeze.   Out would not be hot.

11

Bicky took one bite. . .

Using the things beside his mouth that were called mandibles, Bicky began to chomp on his egg.

and then one more, and one more, until a circle was cut at the top of his egg.

The egg was small,
and the perfect circle was even smaller.
It was tiny to a human eye, but more than big enough,
if judged by a caterpillar's eye.

Bicky took a small pause
to get ready . . .

He was still a little bit afraid to do it;
going out when he had always been in.
But he just had to get through it,
before he was cooked in his skin.

14

. . .then he poked his head out of the shell.

The breeze touched his face right away.
It felt so nice and cool.
Without the thin shell in the way,
Bicky saw the blue sky was really beautiful.

"Not so bad,"
said Bicky.

He had been so afraid,
but now the decision had been made.
He turned his head all about,
and then he climbed right out.

He looked about to see
his egg on a big
green leaf.

The sky was way up high,
because his egg was on the underside.
His leaf was one of many.
He didn't see more eggs on any.

First Bicky thought,
'trying to stay in there
made me hungry.'

Trying 'not to' do what he needed to do
had taken a lot of Bicky's energy.
The rumble in his tummy wasn't new,
it was nature saying "feed me!"

Then Bicky thought, 'this egg looks tasty.'

When he cut the circle in the top of his egg,
his mind had been on the job at hand.
Now he thought about the taste of the egg,
and realized it had been grand.

So Bicky ate his egg;
the one that once was
home.

Eating their egg is what many caterpillars do.
The shell might be small,
but the nutrients it has are good for you,
if you are from within its wall.

Soon it was gone,
but Bicky still
felt hungry.

Even now, Bicky was growing.
Being out of the egg kept that from showing,
because there was nothing to stop him,
from filling out his skin.

The rumbles in his
tiny tummy
got very loud.

At least to Bicky they were very loud.
For a moment he really thought it was a crowd,
that was rumbling in hunger.
The sound seemed more like thunder.

22

"I don't want to eat you," Bicky said to the leaf, "but I am so hungry."

It did not seem to be the thing to do;
eating the plant that was home to you.
Bicky sang a tune or two;
looked around and whistled, too.

"I don't want to eat you," Bicky said again, "but I have to fill my tummy."

The gnawing on Bicky's inside, made him want to eat the leaf outside.

So Bicky began to eat,
. . .

The first bite was a surprise to his mouth,
for Bicky had only eaten egg until now.
The green of the leaf, which he held onto with his feet,
tasted so good, better than he thought it would.

. . . he went on to eat,
and to eat, . . .

Because that is what all caterpillars must do,
chew and chew, until they are through.

26

until he was more than double the size that came out of the egg.

Bicky at double the size!
No surprise that he was totally tired.

"I don't want to rest," said Bicky,

Resting is hard,
because you can't do what you want to do.
Resting means sitting still,
or sleeping until you are renewed.

"and I don't want to change my skin."

He knew it would happen if he took a rest.
He did not believe it was for the best.

But the skin on Bicky
was too tight!
No more food would fit in.

He put up a fight, denying his skin was tight.
But no matter how much he wanted to chew,
he could not eat without room in his skin.

"I don't want to shed my skin, but I must so I can eat more."

It seemed a regular circle;
Bicky wanted to eat more,
but that meant a new skin
would have to grow within.

Bicky took a rest.

It seemed he could not help it;
he became perfectly still.
No moving on his outside,
but lots of hard work inside, . . until. . .

After a night and some shrugs and wiggles,

His old skin wasn't needed.
He spit it at his head.
He shrugged his segments,
until it was shed.

Bicky was out of the old skin and felt the new.

It might look like the old,
but it was soft and stretchy.
Made from the same mold,
it was perfect for Bicky.

34

'How nice to have some room,' Bicky thought.

The new skin was loose, and felt a lot bigger. Bicky could eat a caboose and still have room for dinner.

'I should change my skin as soon as it is taut,' he thought.

There was no denying how much better he felt.
Doing what he needed to do when his skin was tight,
made him feel exactly right.

And so Bicky ate, and shed, four more of his skins.

The time between each change is called instar.
Doing the change sure made Bicky feel like A star!
He looked the same each time, just bigger.

37

By day fourteen, two weeks after opening the egg, Bicky knew it was time.

It had rained, and it had been hot quite a lot.
Weather and season set the reason he had to change.
He could not stay a caterpillar any longer,
But Bicky was still a prolonger.

"I don't want to!"
Bicky yelled at the plant with only one leaf.

He had eaten almost every leaf, but the plant would survive. Nature plans it that way. Creatures rarely destroy a food source.

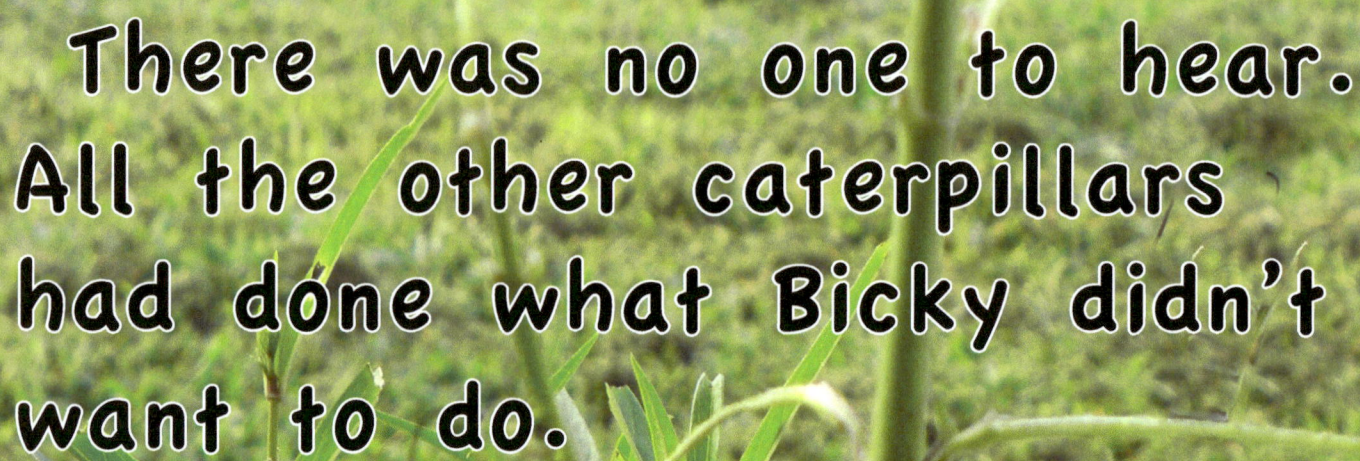

There was no one to hear.
All the other caterpillars
had done what Bicky didn't
want to do.

Even though he never really met them,
and didn't notice them when he was working,
Bicky had known that he wasn't alone.

"I guess I'll have to," said Bicky, "I'm not even hungry anymore."

The time had come .
There was nothing he could do,
except what nature required him to.

41

Off Bicky crawled,
on six real legs, and ten pro-legs,
to find a safe place to hang.

pro-legs

real-legs

His six real legs, up near his mouth, were true insect legs.
His ten pro-legs were supports that were more than pegs.
They had hooks, and with them he could really "book."

Under a blade of grass,
he hung from his bottom,
to look like the letter j .

He was anchored well to the spot,
tied in with his last pro-legs to a dot,
of silk he had spit to that spot.
He settled in and stayed still within.

43

After a day more or less,

Hanging as a J Bicky seemed to be at rest,
but inside his skin things were changing for the best.
A very different kind of skin was about to form,
quite a different uniform.

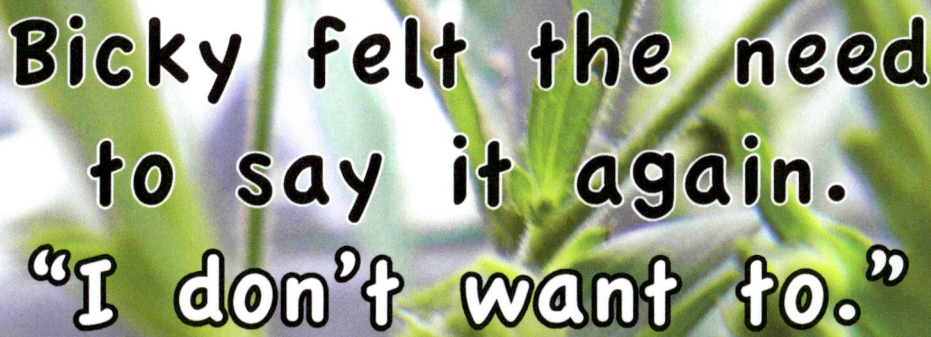

Bicky felt the need
to say it again.
"I don't want to."

The pressure was building in him,
there was no way to stay,
Bicky felt quite grim,
that he would come out in a new way.

Nature took over,
and his last skin was shed

He shrugged it up from his head,
to the silk pad at his last pair of feet.
It gathered there to be shed,
with a wiggle like you do in bed.

to show a chrysalis instead.

The four step process Bicky learned about,
is a change called meta-mor-pho-sis.
That means a different shape comes out,
from nature's chrysalis.

The sun came and went,
day by day until ten had passed,
then he knew it was time.

Again it was the weather and season,
that set the time and gave him reason,
letting him know it was time
to do what he didn't want to do.

"I don't want to!"
Bicky yelled, "I am safe and dry inside this shell."

It made Bicky recall his earlier shell,
the one from which this story began;
it was crowded then, and here as well,
but he was lucky, he had a plan

The weather was just right,
the case turned dark;
then light.

The green of his chrysalis was long gone.
It was now so clear, that everyone near,
could see the wings he was folded upon.

And almost without trying Bicky burst his case and vaulted out.

He had to do it on his own.
His new, long legs held tight while his body fell clear.
He sent fluid from the body that had grown,
into veins that shaped wings for him to steer.

"I don't want to dry out!"
Bicky tried to shout.

It would be an hour before he could leave.
His veins had to harden to support his weight.
HIs wings had to dry.
He could not change the pace.

But wishes don't work,
when nature is in charge.

So Bicky just stayed there.
He waited a bit.
Looking and watching.
Hoping not to be hit.

53

He stretched out his wings, bright orange in the sun.

The sun made his new wings warm,
heating the setae that some call scales.
It felt good to stretch his new kind of arm,
so different from his earlier form.

"That wasn't so bad.
I even had fun."

Bicky liked how it felt.
Never any danger he would melt.
Soon his wings were strong and dry,
Bicky was ready to fly.

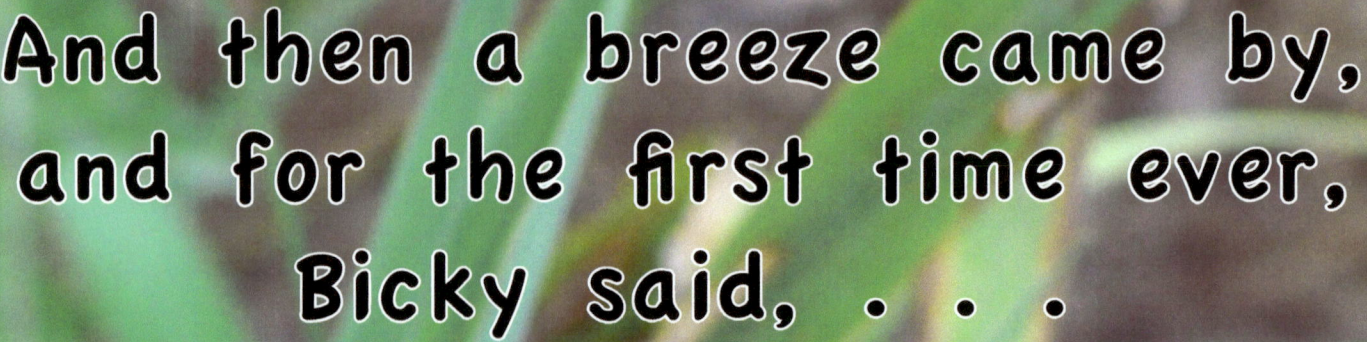

And then a breeze came by,
and for the first time ever,
Bicky said, . . .

"I want to,"
and flew far away.

the

end

of the book,
but not the end of the story,
because Bicky will live for a long while,
migrate with the other monarchs,
and find a mate.

Here is a monarch for you to color.
. . any way you want.

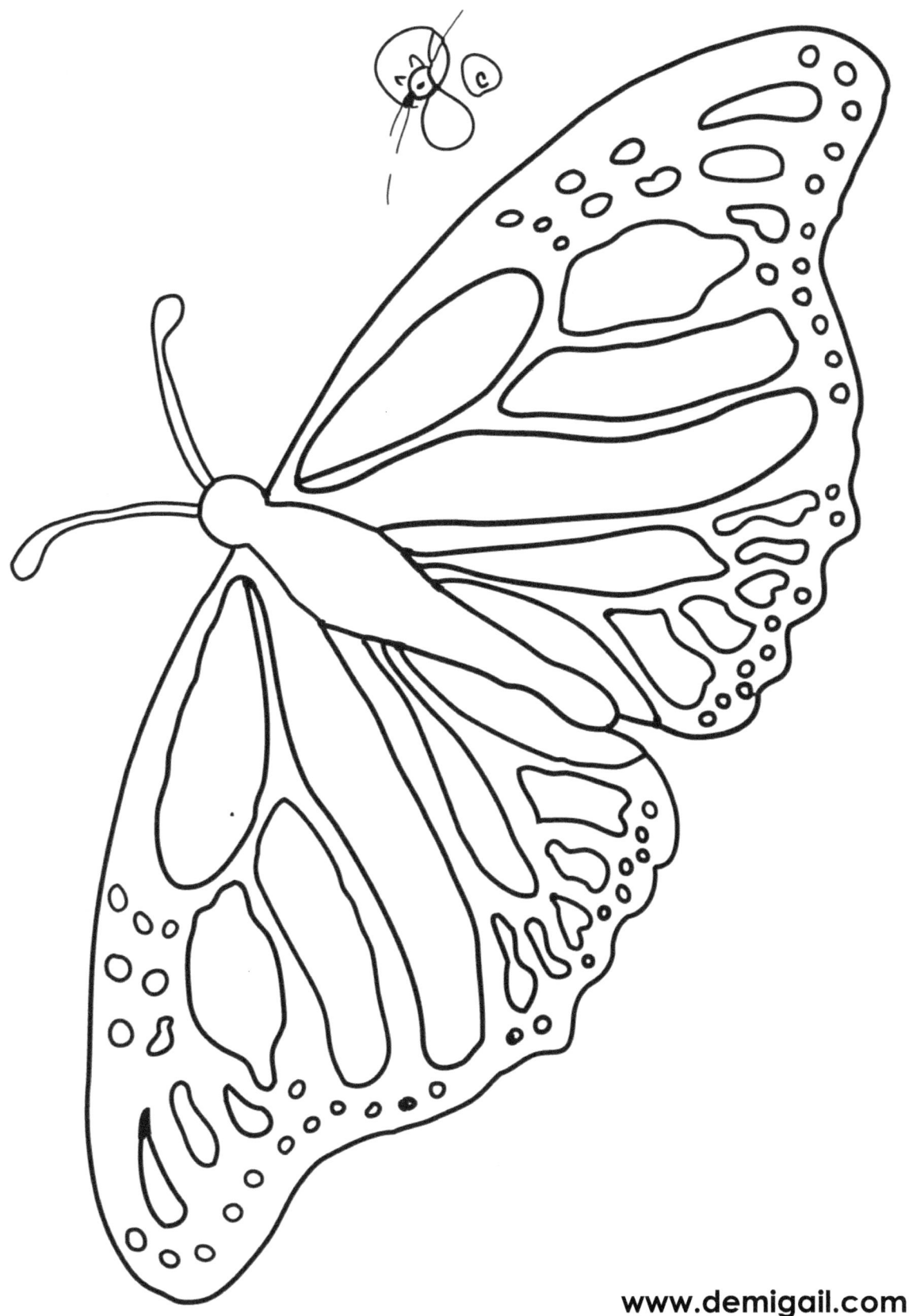

life 'cycle' of Bicky Monarch Butterfly

1. Mother monarch places the elliptical egg very carefully, alone on a leaf, so that the baby inside will have the right food when it comes out. The egg grows from a tiny dot, to be only as big as the cap on the head of a simple straight pin. There are ridges from the top down to the sticky glue that holds the egg tight to the leaf, and tiny bumps with air holes for the baby to breathe by. Unless conditions require the egg to wait longer, (even over winter) it will take between 7 and 14 days until it is time for the baby to emerge by chewing a perfect circle.

2. Bicky pushes his head through and climbs out of the egg to begin his larval stage. Then he eats his old home. Bicky was born to eat a particular kind of plant: a plant toxic to us, and that makes him bad for birds to eat, but wasps, spiders and certain tiny beetles can attack him. He eats and makes waste all day and night, taking a break when he needs to, for weather or to grow a new skin underneath the old one. Each skin stage is called an instar, and Bicky, like most butterfly caterpillars, has five. When he is so full he looks 'stuffed' Bicky spins a pad, clasps it with his hind pro-legs and shrugs out of the old skin to reveal a new, looser fitting one. Monarchs look the same each instar, but some caterpillars look different. When he has grown enough, he wanders away from his host plant to find a safe, sheltered space to hang.

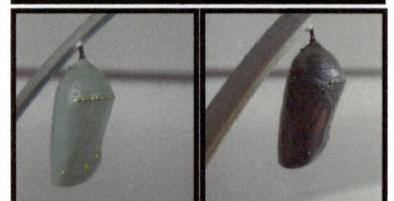

3. The pupa stage is called a chrysalis for a butterfly (a moth has a cocoon). After hanging somewhat still for nearly a day, the old skin splits and is 'shrugged' upward toward his tail end, and then the little chrysalis wiggles wildly to get rid of it. For the next hour, it adjusts itself, drawing upward and compacting itself, and showing its true gold dots. Depending on weather, it will be about 10 days until the shell of the chrysalis thins and becomes clear enough to see the butterfly folded up within it. Bicky breaks out and hangs with a very large body full of fluid that he pumps into the veins of the wings. Then Bicky sits while the veins become rigid and the setae (scales of color) on his wings dry. At this point, Bicky is very vulnerable because he cannot fly. Once dry, however, he opens his wings and takes flight, to do what he must.

male | female

4. When Bicky opens his wings we can see he is male by the two scent glands on his lower wings (the elliptical marks near the veins). He will use these to let female monarchs know he is around because his goal is to find a mate. He is compelled to do it quickly and has enough energy stored that he doesn't need to drink nectar right away. The chewing mouth of the larval stage is gone; now he has a proboscis. This curled appendage is like a drinking straw. When first out of the chrysalis, it is actually two; but it soon fuses together for use in reaching nectar deep in vessel style flowers. Nectar is the only nourishment at this stage; it provides energy and hydration for flying and mating. A monarch can live many months and all monarchs migrate south at winter (but no single monarch goes there and back; they reproduce along the way).

2b **2a** **1** **4**

2c

2d

3a **3b**

Hi young reader and parents!

It has been a lot of fun making this book for you to read! Look and you will see lots of butterflies in your yard or in the park.

In my yard, in the Shenandoah Valley of Virginia, more than 23 different kinds of butterflies visit. There are monarchs of course, but also fritillary, whites, sulphurs, Eastern tiger swallowtails, mourning cloaks, red spotted purples, blues, crescents, snouts, painted ladies, question marks, commas, satyr, buckeyes, spicebush swallowtails, appalachian swallowtails, red admirals, Southern dog-faced, browns, checkerspots, wood nymph, zebra swallowtails, hairstreaks, and all their variations.

I first studied insects when I was at camp as a young girl, then 'caught' them with a net on science field trips in ninth grade. Since 2006, I have been 'catching' butterfly images with my digital cameras. I have done many things with the pictures, like this book and others, but I really like watching the caterpillars and the butterflies to see exactly how they move and do the things they do. You might like to, too!

Though I watch them, and take pictures of them, I don't touch them or interfere with the natural order of things unless I cannot avoid it. So enjoy this book and watch for some butterflies. Tell your own story about what you see to someone, and that will make you a storyteller just like me!

www.ingramcontent.com/pod-product-compliance
Lightning Source LLC
Chambersburg PA
CBHW040306010626
45792CB00025B/1106